Steam Memories: 1950's – 1960's

No. 102: BR Locomotive Works

Southern Region

Copyright Book Law Publications 2018
ISBN 978-1-909625-88-4

INTRODUCTION

The British Railways locomotive workshops located in the Southern Region were far fewer than those on the other regions. There were two main reasons for that situation (a) the SR had far fewer locomotives, be they steam, diesel, or electric, than any other region and (b) under the auspices of the previous ownership's, the various locomotive department had been merged, consolidated and in some cases modernised. The result was that just three workshops served the requirements of the region, Eastleigh which was fairly modern with well laid out shops, next was Ashford which was spacious but did not have of the best layout especially in the erecting shop, whilst Brighton was not only rather cramped, it was also the smallest of the three but was, ironically, chosen by BR to build many of the new Standard locomotives created for the new enterprise.

Ashford, Brighton, and Eastleigh therefore represented the three pre-Grouping entities which made up the Southern Railway and Southern Region at Nationalisation. Ashford dated from 1847 and was the main works of the South Eastern & Chatham Railway eventually combined with the London, Chatham & Dover Railway. Brighton was the oldest of the three workshops under review and dated from 1840 – although 1852 is recognised as the date when it built its first locomotive – with locomotives of the London Brighton & South Coast Railway under its care. Eastleigh was the youngest workshop, not only on the SR but also on BR, and therefore displayed the best layout which in turn took advantage of the methods developed over decades of engineering practice.

Ashford was closed to locomotive overhauls in 1962 with the works being given over to the building and repair of modern freight rolling stock. Brighton closed in 1964 but had been working under a very much reduced workload for a couple of years beforehand. Eastleigh remained involved in locomotive repair and overhaul, taking on the overhaul of electric multiple units too. It survived to the end of BR and passed into private ownership. Our review will look at all three shops during the BR period when steam ruled and when visiting the works could be full of surprise and even mystery.

We would like to thanks the offices of the Armstrong Railway Photographic Trust for the use of images from their archive. Likewise, we thanks the Stour Valley Model Railway Club for the use of photographs from their archive. Finally, a thank you to Chris Dunne for the use of notes from his Father's notebooks which have been very useful in adding some meat to those visits we were lucky enough to do.

David Dunn, Cramlington, October 2018.

(*Frontispiece*)　　**Two preserved locomotives await attention at Eastleigh in October 1959 prior to their incarceration within Clapham Museum. N.W.Skinner (ARPT).**

(*Cover*)　　**See page 54.**

Printed and bound by The Amadeus Press, Cleckheaton, West Yorkshire
First published in the United Kingdom by Book Law Publications, 382 Carlton Hill, Nottingham, NG4 1JA

ASHFORD

On a sunny Saturday 30th April 1960, 'Schools' No.30930 RADLEY comes to the end of its period out of traffic whilst attending Ashford shops during a heavy overhaul. A repaint is next then it's back home to Bricklayers Arms shed to join the other seven 'Schools' still resident at that depot. Only two years earlier 73B was home to seventeen of the class but the expanding SR electrification network was taking traffic away from steam traction and forcing SR steam locomotives into the scrapyards at an ever increasing rate. Ashford works had taken responsibility for these 4-4-0s for years but many of them were now receiving their last major overhauls whilst others were soon to be cut-up! *Duncan Hagan (ARPT)*.

The main erecting shop at Ashford on 30th April 1960 with the usual SR customers and a surprise in the shape of WR 'Pannier' No.4656; the 0-6-0PT was at that time allocated to the Southern Region shed at 72C Yeovil. She wasn't the only former GWR engine working on the Region during the late 1950s/early 1960s. Nine Elms had a number of Pannier's on the books with Nos.4634, 4672, 4681, 4692, and 4698; Wadebridge had Nos.4666 and 4694 resident whilst Yeovil looked after No.4689. Weymouth too had three on the books with Nos.4624, 4688 and 8799 residing. The shed with the most and the shed which might be the least expected to have any was nearby Folkestone which housed six of them thus: 4601, 4610, 4616, 4626, 4630, and 4631. *Duncan Hagan (ARPT).*

Thursday 4th May 1967 and the former locomotive works at Ashford had been changed into a wagon works with building and repairs to BR's modernised fleet of air-braked and higher capacity wagon fleet. Many of the so-called Freighliner wagons were built here long before the service was rolled out by BR as the future of wagon-load traffic. This view of the yard shows two old steam locomotives in amongst the various new wagons being turned-out at the workshop. Ashford dealt with 250 locomotives during 1960 but in 1961 this figure was down to 100 with even less locomotive work planned for the following year. The *Railway Observer* reported that on 27th April 1962 the following locomotives were receiving either Casual or Intermediate repairs, General overhauls having already ceased in March: 31637, 31796, 31799, 31823, 31845, 31879, 80066. From 24th March to 21st April the following locomotives constituted the last examples scrapped at Ashford: 30804, 30900, 30909, 31530, 31689, 31721, 32509, 32581, and 32588, virtually in that order! From July locomotive repairs had virtually ceased at Ashford and during that month a couple of steam cranes had arrived for overhaul whilst the occasional steam locomotive called in for minor attention. *K.Gregory (ARPT)*.

We are still looking around the works on that first Thursday in April 1967 and this area of the site, though a sight for sore eyes for many was hardly fitting for a workshop trying to modernise its image from one of Victorian engineering to high-end modern contemporary engineering. This was a Stationary Boiler providing steam to goodness knows which part or process within the works but although welcome to steam enthusiasts everywhere, the near-sixty-three year old relic was hardly what BR's top brass wanted. The incumbent 0-6-0 was former SECR Wainwright 0-6-0 No.31271 which was a product of these very workshops being put into traffic in December 1904 but now it was hardly welcome even though it was still working for a living. Renumbered DS240 in the SR Departmental Service locomotive scheme in July 1963, the C class was eventually retired and by the end of 1967 it was apparently cut-up on site at Ashford, a fitting end perhaps to a long-time resident which came home. *K. Gregory (ARPT)*.

An undated image of DS240 this time up against the Erecting shop wall; was it ready for the chop? It doesn't appear so and is not only connected to the system, it's also making steam. The ground area of Ashford works covered just over 26 acres of which eight and a half acres were covered by the workshops. Locomotive repair ceased here in 1962 with wagon building taking precedence from there on. Note the new Freightliner wagon in the foreground - B602046 – a 51-ton bogie vehicle with a building date plated as 1964 which would coincide with this image. *A.R. Thompson collection (ARPT).*

One of the 'Yanks' doing some work; this is DS238 which was one of six 'USA' class 0-6-0T surviving from Running Stock into Departmental Service Stock (DS233–DS238). Being relatively young compared with most SR shunting locomotives, these twenty-odd year 'youngsters' were still useful and required little in the way of maintenance like some of the older locomotives. Formerly No.30070, this tank was renumbered in August 1963 and worked here in Ashford Wagon shops until September 1967. Besides DS238, Ashford was also home to DS237 (30065). The other four USA tanks were widely scattered with DS233 (30061) at Redbridge Sleeper Depot; DS234 (30062) at Meldon Quarry; and DS235 (30066) with DS236 (30074) working at Lancing Carriage Works. *K.Gregory (ARPT)*.

Alongside the old Pattern Store at the eastern end of the Locomotive works was a dead-end siding on which items 'pending' were placed away from the main activity of the workshops. On 13th April 1957 D class 4-4-0 No.31737 was one such item which had been withdrawn six months earlier and was slated for preservation. Built at Ashford in November 1901, the former South Eastern & Chatham engine was one of those which resided inside Clapham Museum long before the NRM opened its doors in 1975. *F.W.Hampson (ARPT).*

Yet another SB at Ashford; this particular example was hiding its identity but nevertheless it looks to be in something of a predicament and ready for the chop. The date is 10th May 1953 and the six-coupled engine was still connected to the heating system. Note the independent snowplough tucked-in behind that tender. *K.H.Cockerill (ARPT)*.

Dover (74C) based O1 No.31065 was another Ashford product from SE&CR days. Stabled outside the Erecting shop on 1st July 1961, the 0-6-0 had just been withdrawn with a view to preservation. *F.W.Hampson (ARPT)*.

'Schools' No.30929 MALVERN was sent into works for attention to its axleboxes; which ones is unknown but the 4-4-0 seen here on 1st July 1961 steamed off the premises after attention later in the summer. However, on the scrap road a month later were sisters Nos.30904, 30914, 30932, 30933, 30938, and 30939, all nameless and most of them condemned but No.30933 was still awaiting a decision! *F.W.Hampson (ARPT)*.

With just a few tweaks to the painting of the front end, and the highlighting of that numberplate, U class No.31791 basks in the sun at Ashford on Monday 18th April 1960. The engines of this class in the number group 31790 to 31809 were originally 2-6-4Ts known as Class K and all carried names of rivers; our engine was RIVER ADUR before it was rebuilt to a 2-6-0 tender engine in 1928. BR classified these engines in the 4MT range but in 1954 they were reclassified 4P3F. Allocated to 72C Yeovil for most of its BR life, the 2-6-0 had been transferred to 71A Eastleigh during its absence away at shops. It was amongst the last of the SR 2-6-0s being withdrawn in June 1966, the last of its class! Sixty years old C class No.31686 looks on from the rear; it was in for minor repairs which would see it back into traffic for a couple of years afterwards. *Duncan Hagan (ARPT)*.

13

Three months later on 16th July 1960, ex-LBSC 0-6-2T No.32487 from Class E4 was completing a major overhaul and was out in the sunshine being got ready for its return to traffic. *Duncan Hagan (ARPT).*

Locomotives arriving at Ashford for shopping during the period Tuesday 27th March to Tuesday 24th April 1951 were as follows:

A1X:	32644	L1:	31759
C:	31243, 31461, 31582, 31681,	N:	31814, 31835, 31857,
C2X:	32536	O1:	1041, 31383,
D1:	31494, 31505, 31727,	P:	31557
E3:	32458	Q1:	33008
E4:	32467, 32486, 32508	R1:	1174, 1335, 1339,
E6:	32413	R:	31670
H:	S1544	U:	31628
J:	31595	U1:	31897
L:	31777	WD 8F:	77150

Under construction: 10202, 15228, and 15229.

On Saturday 6th October 1951 the following were undergoing overhauls, repair or construction at Ashford works:

C:	31054, 31219, 31695, 1711,	N:	31404, 31414, 31813, 31821, 31857, 31869,
D:	31577	Q1:	33018
D1:	31494, 31505, 31739,	R:	31662, 31671,
E4:	32503, 32579, 32581,	U:	31634, 31636, 31639, 31803,
E4X:	32478	U1:	31893,
E6:	2408, 32415,	W:	31915
H:	31164, 31520,	WD 8F:	90267
L1:	31756	0-6-0DE:	15232 (under construction).

A nice little snippet from 1951 concerned a member of the fairly new – then – 'Britannia' class Pacifics thus: The first of its class to visit Ashford locomotive works, 'Britannia' Pacific No.70004 WILLIAM SHAKESPEARE was still in the shops on Monday 5th November 1951 after fracturing a side rod whilst working the Up *GOLDEN ARROW* at speed on Sunday 21st October! This 73A Stewarts Lane Pacific had previously taken part in the South Bank Exhibition and had just started regular working on the Pullman train from 11th October. Ashford accepted the locomotive on the day of the incident. No.70004 left the works at Ashford on an unknown date but was back on its 73A duty from Monday 10th December. Afterwards No.70004 became a regular attraction at the Eastleigh Locomotive Works open days up to its transfer to the London Midland Region on 21st June 1958. No.70004 never returned to Ashford and was probably the only one of the class to visit the Kentish workshop.

BRIGHTON

RCTS

32425

75A

We start off our Brighton sequence with this view of H Class 'Atlantic' No.32425 TREVOSE HEAD at the head of an RCTS Pullman special in platform 7 at Brighton (Central) station on Sunday 19th October 1952. The train was the second of two such specials – the other ran a fortnight earlier on Sunday 5th October with No.32424 BEACHY HEAD in charge – organised by the Railway Correspondence & Travel Society to celebrate the Centenary of Brighton Locomotive Works. Both trains consisted of eight cars of Pullman stock – numbered 17, 31, 35, 60, 61, 98, 99, and 208 but not in that order – which left London (Victoria) at 10-14 a.m. on each date, hauled by a former London, Brighton & South Coast Railway 'Atlantic' headed for Brighton with arrival approximately one hour later. About 284 passengers travelled on each train and coffee was served en route to Brighton whilst afternoon tea was a treat on the return journey, all provided by the Pullman Car Company. This view shows the works offices on the left with signs of extensions to the original building. No.32425 had earlier posed on the No.3 road at the north end of the works but was now coupled to the train ready for the 50.9 miles run back to London. *K.H.Cockerill (ARPT)*.

The southern end of the Erecting shop at Brighton on 19th October 1952 with a horde of gabardine and Burberry – the uniform of the period – clad RCTS members sampling the delights of the workshop! It was just about here where locomotives of the ill-fated 'Leader' class were built but on this date more conventional steam locomotives were in attendance for overhaul. Locomotive building finished here in March 1957 and repairs finished in 1958. Note that there wasn't a hard-hat or conspicuity vest in sight on this occasion! Locomotives inside the works on this date were Steam: C class 31102, 31227, 31579, 31683, E3 class 32170, K class 32353, E6 class 32409, E4 class 32507, 32511, C2X class 32548, E5 class 2573, Class 4MT 42070, BR Standard Class 4MT 80049 nearly complete, 80050 boiler fitted, 80051 frames laid, 80052 frames ready. Two diesel-electric locomotives were also resident: BR 350 h.p. 0-6-0DE shunters 15216 and 15230. *K.H.Cockerill (ARPT)*.

As eluded too in the Introduction to this album, Brighton works, with its early opening date of 1852, was victim to expansion within the town and was hemmed-in by early development around the centre of Brighton. It was even bereft of good road access and although it had the highest proportion of covered accommodation of all the BR works – with 77.8% of the nine acre site covered by workshops – it had no chance of expanding itself and was regarded in BR days as not worth the cost of modernising, even in a limited fashion. Strange then that Brighton was responsible for building 130 of the 155 BR Standard Class 4 2-6-4T locomotives, Derby (15), and Doncaster (10) were responsible for the balance. One interesting fact concerning these mixed-traffic tank engines is the costs with regard to different batches thus: No.80010 built July 1951 with an estimated cost of £11,025 but an actual official cost of £15,277; No.80078 built February 1954 with an estimated cost of £14,400 and an actual official cost of £17,324; No.80105 built April 1955 with an estimated cost of £14,400 and an actual official cost of £18,206; and finally No.80154 built March 1957 at an estimated cost of £18,100 and an actual official cost of £21,944, nearly twice the original estimate for No.80010. However, six years had passed, inflation was a factor but that was low compared with later – and earlier – periods in the UK economic history. Certain components had changed and others introduced for various batches to hike up the costs.

Another remarkable building feat carried out at Brighton works was the five-and-half-years between May 1945 and January 1951 when they produced all but six of the 110 so-called 'Light Pacifics' of the Bulleid 'West Country/Battle of Britain' class. During that period from No.21C101 (34001) being put into traffic and its sister No.34110 being completed, Brighton was responsible for erecting the Pacifics, and producing all the components except the tenders which were built at Ashford. Bogies, brake gear, cabs, cylinders, and other minor components were the responsibility of Eastleigh, the works responsible for building the half dozen examples which completed the class thus: Nos.34095 (10/49), 34097 (11/49), 34099 (12/49), 34101 (2/50), 34102 (3/50), and 34104 (4/50). In 1946 alone, Brighton turned-out thirty-one WC Pacifics which was another feat in itself considering all else which was taking place within the works. One slight mystery concerning No.34110 is the release date to traffic as late January 1951, nearly eight months after the penultimate engine No.34109. There was speculation that the BB was to be fitted with all sorts of experimental devices but in the event 66 SQUADRON was no different to the others class members released in 1950.

Of course, Brighton was doing other things during the period of Pacific construction such as overhauling other locomotives, scrapping the old and worn-out, and producing some memorable but undistinguished steam locomotives in the shape of Bulleid's 'Leader' class. Five had been ordered but only four – Nos.36001– 36004 – of the 100-ton, six-cylinder, 0-6-6-0T were built, and all at Brighton in 1949. They were doomed from the moment the first and only one – 36001 – was steamed in June 1949. Though never becoming BR stock, that single engine ran trials until November 1950 after which it was allowed to rot until cut up at Eastleigh during the week ending 12th May 1951. No.36002 was completed but never apparently steamed. No.36003 was virtually complete, whereas No.36004 was only half-built. Of the others, all but 36002 were also scrapped in May 1951 at Brighton, whilst No.36002 followed in July to bring to an end one inglorious class which never was of any use anyway!

During 1950 and 1951, amidst the production of all things Southern, Brighton was given the job of building a batch – 42066 to 42106 – of ex-LMS Fairburn designed Class 4 mixed-traffic 2-6-4Ts for the Southern Region. These were a prelude to the BR Standard six-coupled tanks begun in 1951 and the first of them, 42096 appeared in July 1950 whilst the last, 42095 was turned-out in June 1951 which coincided nicely with the first BR version being ready for traffic the following month.

Starting in late June 1945 Brighton took in dozens of WD 'Austerity' 2-8-0s from 'dumps' located in southern England. The locomotives were meant for working freight trains on the Southern Railway and all eighty-seven of the engines were given Heavy General or Heavy Intermediate overhauls prior to being put into traffic. A few only required Light Intermediate repairs but nevertheless Brighton took care of them before and after Nationalisation. That particular job finished in February 1950 by which time the works had started to overhaul the SR allocated members of the class as a matter of course. During the early days of BR, they even took in a number of the 2-10-0 'Austerities' bound for the Scottish Region. Brighton did and certainly could tackle any job given to them. In that early BR period the works was taking in an average of ten locomotives a month and these ranged from Pacifics to ex-LMS Cl.4 tanks to diesel shunting locomotives.

Just before we change motive power, we must mention one of Brighton's wartime exploits whereby they built a large number of Stanier 8F 2-8-0s during WW2. These were tackled in 1943 and 1944 and their number groups were as follows: 8613-8617, 8625-8649, 8663-8670, 8675-8704. Ashford (14) and Eastleigh (23) were also involved with this venture but compared with Brighton's efforts they lagged behind somewhat.

As mentioned previously, Ashford was responsible for the construction of a handful of diesel locomotives during the transition period from Southern Railway to British Railways ownership. In March 1954 Brighton turned out its one and only diesel-electric No.10203, the final example of a trio of 2-6-6-2 (1-Co-Co-1) main-line locomotives designed by the Southern Railway and powered by an English-Electric 16SVT Mk.2 prime mover producing 2,000hp. After a very brief period in traffic working from Nine Elms, 10203 was taken to the International Railway Congress Exhibition being held in the roundhouse at Willesden motive power depot. Thereafter it entered traffic full-time on the Waterloo–Exeter passenger services. No.10203 was 'spotted' outside Brighton works on 16th May 1954 ready to have its black livery 'bulled-up' for the Willesden 'do' some nine days later. One of Brighton's Cl.4 tanks – 80084 – was in attendance at Willesden having been hauled there from Brighton by 10203. Meanwhile, also in attendance at Brighton works on that Sunday in May was one of the ex-LMS twins 10001 (actually the BR-built member of the pair dating from July 1948 and like 10000 was allocated at this time in its life to the Southern Region working out of Waterloo), and 1937 SR vintage 0-6-0DE shunter 15202 from Norwood Junction depot.

Finally, Brighton also tended to the requirements of the SR's electric locomotive fleet but they were small fry compared with the others!
Stabled on Brighton shed that 16th day of May 1954 were: A1X: 32640; C2X: 32437, 32438, 32440, 32442; D3: 32390; E1: 31497; E1/R: 32695; E3: 32165, 32166, 32167, 32169, 32170; E4: 32485, 32513, 32514, 32515, 32518, 32577; E5: 32583; H: 31310; H2: 32421 SOUTH FORELAND, 32424 BEACHY HEAD; K: 32337, 32338, 32339, 32341, 32342, 32348; M7: 30053; N: 31829, 31874; P: 31325, 31556, 31558; Q: 30544; WC/BB: 34045 OTTERY ST MARY, 34047 CALLINGTON, 34048 CREDITON, 34067 TANGMERE, 34104 BERE ALSTON; Z: 30950; Ex-LMS Cl.4: 42087, 42090, 42103, 42104, 42105; BR Standard Cl.4: 80016, 80017, 80019, 80033, 80083 (new).

Total 51.

Appearing as diminutive as ever, A1X No.32635 was stabled on Brighton shed yard 17th September 1961. This six-coupled tank had a somewhat interesting identification history starting work in June 1878 as No.35 and also carrying the name MORDEN. It later became No.635, then 2635. Just prior to Nationalisation it was transferred to the Southern's Service locomotive listing and became 377S and was employed at Brighton Works. Under Departmental charge, it was renumbered DS377 but in 1959 the 0-6-0T was returned to Capital Stock and became No.32635, all the time wearing the LBSCR yellow livery. Withdrawn in March 1963, this was one A1X which didn't attract the preservationist's attention and was scrapped later that year. Note the height of those lamp irons. *I.S.Jones (ARPT).*

No.32635 when it was Service locomotive 377S. Note the somewhat interesting coupling and plumbing gear around the front end! This image was recorded on 19th October 1952 outside the Smiths Shop with the Accounting Department forming the background. On the first date of the RCTS Centenary visits – 5th October 1952 – this 0-6-0T posed in this condition with 'Atlantic' No.32424 on No.3 road at the north end of the works site. *P.J.Robinson (ARPT)*.

Okay, so we have a soft-spot for 32635. Here she is as DS377 and looking rather smart in that LBSC livery on 1st May 1958. Her work here was nearly done, and as the locomotive works wound down the A1X would be returned to Capital stock. Brighton was responsible for building all of Stroudley's A1 class from which these A1X class six-coupled tanks derived; ten of them were eventually preserved which by any means is a good average for a class consisting of just a dozen Capital stock locomotives and two in Service stock at Nationalisation! *L.Turnbull (ARPT).*

No.32635 on Brighton shed with nothing to do. The faded glory of its previous employment is plain to see but that job had now disappeared. The tank never received a front numberplate and it is arguable that it was ever cleaned again either so this is the condition which saw its demise and eventual oblivion. Perhaps it was those coal guards on the bunker which put people off its potential as an attraction somewhere. *Ian H. Hodgson (ARPT).*

Just as a change, we now feature A1X No.32636 which was employed on that third Sunday in October 1952 running the RCTs enthusiasts on a two-coach push-pull set (No.727, ex-LBSCR, brought in from Gillingham for the occasion) shuttle service between Brighton and the branch to Kemp Town. On each Sunday the little 0-6-0T ran three services to cater for all the RCTS members including those who joined the festivities at Brighton. Once sold out of railway service, the A1X was taken back by the Southern in 1927 and never really looked back; withdrawn in November 1963, No.32636 was chosen for preservation. *K.H.Cockerill (ARPT)*.

An undated photograph of WD 2-10-0 'Austerity' No.90766 stabled on Brighton shed yard after a visit to the adjacent Works. Note that although the BR number has been applied along with a coat of black paint, there is no BR emblem or any lettering proclaiming ownership. However, this particular locomotive was renumbered from 73790 to 90766 in May 1949 when Brighton was also dealing with the ex-WD 2-8-0s destined for the Southern Region. No.90766 departed for the Scottish Region and was allocated to Motherwell shed from 9th July 1949. *Norman Preedy.*

EASTLEIGH

So when did the fuel-oil debacle finish on the Southern Region? Sparked initially by the fact that coal supplies were going to be badly disrupted during the latter years of the Big Four and the early years of BR's existence, the railway companies with government assistance decided to invest heavily on oil fired locomotives. The actual burning of the oil in existing fire boxes did not present much of a problem and hundreds of locomotives on all four of the Grouped companies were converted ready for the big switch over to oil. Tenders were fitted out with new tanks located in the coal bunker space whilst supply of the oil at the depots caused the biggest headaches with storage tanks, heating boilers and associated pipework all requiring space and new building installations at the depots. The Southern Railway appears not to have been as enthusiastic as the others in preparing for the changeover to oil; a smaller steam locomotive fleet meant less of a challenge to keep traffic moving in the event of a coal crisis although the Railway's reliance on electricity was in any way a somewhat doubtful ideal as all the electricity then consumed by the Southern was produced in coal-fired generating stations. In the event the crisis passed without any need to call upon the oil suppliers and those locomotives that had been converted were put into store to await conversion back to coal firing or were sent to the scrap yards as surplus. On an unknown date in 1950 three L11s – with No.30411 nearest – stand forlornly at Eastleigh works waiting for the call which never came. Eight L11, all with eight-wheel tenders, were converted and all were scrapped by June 1952 without reverting back to coal. Ten T9s were also converted, all with the larger 8-wheel tender; all of those had been withdrawn by May 1951. On the other hand five N15s which had been converted for oil were all converted back to coal by September 1948. A single N class – 31831 – and a pair of U class had been converted but they too reverted back to coal firing in 1948. Finally, two Bulleid 'Light Pacifics' – 34019 and 34036 – were also converted in 1947 but were soon altered back to coal burning. No tank engines were involved. *Trevor J. Saunders (ARPT).*

Eastleigh summer 1950; converted L11 No.30157 became BR property but never turned a wheel in revenue earning service. It was finally condemned in March 1952 and scrapped shortly afterwards. *Trevor J. Saunders (ARPT)*.

'Leader' No.36001 near the coaling stage at Eastleigh shed on an unknown date during its trial period. The only member of the class to actually perform any substantial testing, No.36001 was looking far from smart on this particular day. The only one of the four broken up at Eastleigh works, 36001 had been left to rot after trials were concluded in November 1950 and the locomotive never steamed again. This image probably dates from 1950 as 36001 had been active since June 1949. Scrapping took place in May 1951. *Trevor J. Saunders (ARPT).*

Since its return from the Isle-of-Wight in 1946, A1X No.2678 had been on loan to the Kent & East Sussex Railway but at Nationalisation BR transferred it to Ashford (74A) and later, in 1954, to St Leonards (74E). Fratton (70F) was home to a number of the diminutive six-coupled tanks with approximately five or six serving the Hayling Island branch from Havant and in the of spring 1958 No.32678 joined them for an eighteen month stint before it continued its westward advance to Eastleigh (71A) shed. This undated image shows No.32678 receiving a thorough Intermediate overhaul amongst the Pacific tenders. *K.H.Cockerill (ARPT).*

At 7-35 a.m. on Saturday 9th May 1964 the East Midlands branch of the RCTS set off from Nottingham (Victoria) on their *EAST MIDLANDER* No.7 railtour. The destination for this tour was Eastleigh and then Swindon, the motive power for the longest leg of the journey was 'Duchess' No.46251 CITY OF NOTTINGHAM which took the 12-coach train with its 500 plus passengers to Didcot where 'West Country' No.34038 LYNTON took over for the journey to Eastleigh via the Didcot, Newbury & Southampton line where a speed restriction of 30 m.p.h. was in force. At Eastleigh station the Pacific came off and USA 0-6-0T No.30071 was coupled up to the 400-ton train for the short leg into the works yard. This is the view from coach No.4 as the special is wheeled into the works yard by robust No.30071. *Ian H. Hodgson (ARPT).*

The hordes from Nottingham descend from their carriages and begin their reconnoitre of the Eastleigh workshops and yards. The USA tank doesn't look too clever and its livery on this date was described by more than one observer as a shade of grey. No.30073 was the preferred motive power but that was apparently unavailable for technical reasons! *Ian H. Hodgson (ARPT).*

LYNTON is coupled onto the RCTS special and the event is recorded on film by virtually everybody who travelled on the train. The driver and fireman were certainly basking in the limelight as they prepare No.34038 for the circuitous route through Hampshire and Wiltshire. *K. H. Cockerill (ARPT).*

Immaculate! A last pose by the 'Spam Can' prior to departure from Eastleigh; it was then on to Swindon via Romsey, Salisbury, Westbury and Chippenham. 'Duchess' No.46251 was waiting at Swindon engine shed to return the special to Nottingham. The weather on the day was perfect and 500 plus happy members and friends certainly enjoyed an outing to remember. *Ian H. Hodgson (ARPT)*.

Remember A1X No.32635 at Brighton? Well here she is at Eastleigh on Saturday 20th April 1963 just a few weeks after being condemned. She has been sent to the former LSWR works for cutting-up and is already showing signs of being prepared for the scrapyard having lost its chimney – where did that go? The coupling rods would have been removed at Brighton prior to transit and they can be seen secured to the front running plate. The rain does nothing to lessen the gloom and the old girl looks considerably messed-up compared with previous images recorded at Brighton. When the deed of breaking up the 0-6-0T was completed or even commenced is unknown but it was certainly carried out during 1963. *George Ives.*

It appears that the chimneys go first! On that same damp Saturday 'Schools' No.30916 ex-WHITGIFT and No.30911 ex-DOVER, still with its chimney, also await their fate in the scrapyard at Eastleigh. *A .Ives (ARPT)*.

Adams G6 No.30238 was taken into Departmental stock – or Service Stock as the SR preferred – in November 1960 but by December 1962 they had condemned the 0-6-0T and it was taken to Eastleigh for scrapping where on 20th April 1963 it was stabled awaiting the deed. No.30238 had spent much of the BR period working from Guildford shed (70C) having worked the early years at Salisbury (72B) and then a few weeks at Reading (70E) during the autumn of 1950. Its last place of work was at Meldon Quarry, the SR's own stone source for the ballast used on the tracks throughout the region. Having replaced another G6 at the quarry, No.30238 was renumbered DS 682 at Guildford shed before working direct to Devon and its new home at Meldon. DS 682 was itself replaced by USA 0-6-0T No.30062 which acquired the Departmental number DS 234 and which worked the quarry until early 1967 when a diesel shunter took over. Now then, can anyone kindly enlighten us locomotive aficionados as to what kind of hopper that vehicle is behind the G6? *George Ives*

DS 3152 the locomotive replaced by No.30238 aka DS 682. This image was recorded in the scrapyard at Eastleigh on 21st August 1960, some three months before the other G6 took up the cudgel at Meldon Quarry. Note the rather neat sign writing on the tank side proclaiming that this locomotive worked for the *Engineers Dept. Meldon Quarry*. Recruited as a service locomotive in June 1950, this 0-6-0T was intended to be numbered 30272 by BR but in the event it kept its Southern Railway number 272 until it crossed over! The question now is what locomotive stood in for this G6 during its absence from Meldon until DS 682 turned up in November 1960? *C. J .B .Sanderson (ARPT).*

The scrap men take a closer look at their handiwork on the front end of N15 No.30779 – formerly SIR COLGREVANCE – being dismantled in September 1959. In the background another N15 is being tentatively prepared for a similar fate. *A.R. Thompson (ARPT).*

Further scenes in the scrapyard as an M7 – No.30028 – begins the process of disappearing on 6th October 1962. It appears that the unidentified O2 behind has spent some time as a Stationary Boiler somewhere. *C.J.B. Sanderson (ARPT).*

You didn't think an album about Southern Region locomotive works wasn't going to include a lot of images illustrating the A1X class did you? This is No.32661 looking less than smart at Eastleigh on Sunday 23rd June 1963. Late of Eastleigh shed, and Fratton beforehand, the little 0-6-0T had been withdrawn during the previous April. This view shows the tank in its final form with black fully lined livery complete with 0P power classification. Note also the lamp iron arrangement at this end; have some irons been removed!? Sister No.32635 is buffered up but they'll be no safety-in-numbers here as both locomotives were broken up just weeks later. Now, is it just coincidence or what? Both engines have bunker extensions whereas all those preserved examples did not! *F.W. Hampson (ARPT)*.

The same Sunday visit in June 1963 found 'Schools' No.30934 also waiting for a slot in the scrapyard. Formerly named ST. LAWRENCE, this 4-4-0 was a product of Eastleigh – to traffic March 1935 – and had been modified with a Lemaitre multiple-jet blast pipe but that was no defence against withdrawal. No.30934 was amongst the final seventeen which were condemned in December 1962. The distinctive sloping inwards of the cab side sheets and tender sides which enabled the class to be used on the Hastings line are clearly visible. Note the Tiger Moth above the dome on its way to Southampton Airport. *F.W.Hampson (ARPT)*.

Okay, this one is for the modellers. They'll be no more after this. A1X DS681 – formerly No.32659 and latterly working at Lancing carriage works – in the scrapyard at Eastleigh just days away from oblivion! Have a good look at all those detail differences so that whenever you build or acquire a model of one of these little gems you have no excuse to get anything wrong with the super-detailing. Finally, note that bunker extension!!! *F.W.Hampson (ARPT)*.

We've gone forward in time to 16th April 1966 and by now Eastleigh is scrapping some of the Southern Region diesel shunter fleet, or so it would appear. The coupled wheelset in the foreground complete with reduction gear and Bulleid-style boxpok wheels could have been something of a 'red-herring' whereas the former-GWR 2-8-0 – No.2818 – was laid-up having been withdrawn in October 1963 and was now awaiting preservation. *K. Gregory (ARPT).*

Wearing the lined black livery applied by British Railways, Ramsgate based 'Schools' No.30922 MARLBOROUGH sits in the yard at Eastleigh ready for a visit to the shops on 7th May 1955. Latterly of Bricklayers Arms (73B), St. Leonards (74E), Dover (74C), Brighton (75A), Stewarts Lane (73A), and Ramsgate (74B), the 4-4-0 was not one of the twenty-one chosen to be fitted with the Lemaitre multiple-jet blast pipe incorporating a wide chimney. Withdrawn in November 1961, the 'V' was scrapped shortly afterwards. *F.W. Hampson (ARPT).*

N15X 'Remembrance' No.32328 HACKWORTH had been withdrawn in February 1955 in on 7th May 1955 the 4P is getting nearer to the scrapyard and oblivion. No.32328 was one of those N15Xs loaned to the Great Western during WW2 along with sisters 32327, 32329, 32331, and 32332. Of LBSCR origin, these engines started life in 1914 as 4-6-4 tank engines of Class L for working express passenger trains. All seven were rebuilt between 1934 and 1936 as 4-6-0s coupled to 8-wheel tenders. No.32338 was the first of them to be condemned; No.32330 was the last some two years and five months later. *F.W. Hampson (ARPT).*

Was this its first Southern overhaul for this locomotive? USA 0-6-0T No.63 receives attention at Eastleigh on 12th August 1947. *A.R. Clark (ARPT).*

Stanier 8F No.48774 stables at Eastleigh works on an unknown date in the summer of 1957 shortly after being welcomed into the BR fold along with sisters Nos.48773, and 48775. All three had received minor overhauls, painting and renumbering after their military service. This former War Department 2-8-0 was numbered 70320 in the WD scheme but in 1952 it was renumbered 501. Returned to the UK from the Middle East (Suez) in July 1952 with four other WD Stanier 8F 2-8-0s, No.320 along with sisters 307, 508, 575, and 583 were all taken to BR's Derby locomotive works for refurbishment; their condition was essentially deplorable with many parts missing. Although it was some time before the first of the WD engines (their tenders – or those intended for them – came back on a different freighter a some three years later) was overhauled at Derby, the rest followed into the shops by 1955 and then they were returned to the WD, three of them – 307, 320 and 583, all renumbered in 1952 to 500, 501, 512 – were sent to Longmoor military railway whilst the other two went to Military Port No.2 at Cairnryan. It was the Longmoor 'three' which became BR property in 1957. Our subject here became BR No.90743, then 90734 before finally becoming 48774 in the Stanier 8F fleet. Purchased from the Ministry of Supply, the trio were accepted into BR stock in September 1957 and all three allocated to Polmadie. The Cairnryan engines were scrapped in 1959 as surplus to WD requirements. *K.H. Cockerill (ARPT)*.

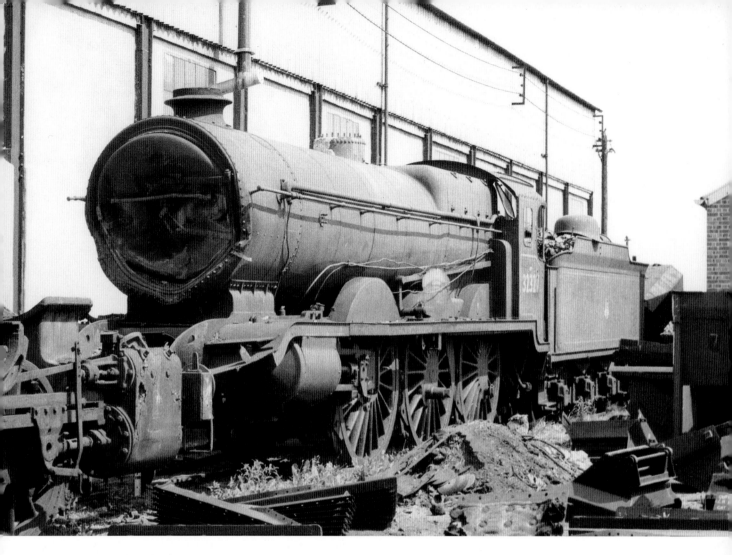

'Remembrance' No.32327 TREVITHICK languishes at Eastleigh in 1956 after being withdrawn in January 1956. The locomotive had received its front-end damage in a collision on 23rd December 1955 when hauling a passenger train it ran into the back of another train at Woking. These engines were rebuilds from 4-6-4 tank engines built for the LB&SCR from 1914 to 1922, and rebuilt by the SR into 4-6-0 tender engines during 1934-36. Entering BR life in Southern Malachite green livery, the seven engines in this class were all changed to BR lined-black. Classified N15X, they were rated as 4P in the power classification table and even during Southern Railway days were working secondary passenger services. BR continued those duties and all seven were allocated to Basingstoke shed hauling cross-country and inter-regional services. Two were withdrawn in 1955, four in 1956 including our subject here, and No.32331 became the last one before it too was condemned in July 1957. None were preserved. *(ARPT)*.

After its last General overhaul, M7 No.30320 is ready to return to its home shed at Nine Elms on Sunday 26th June 1960. Remember that hopper wagon query earlier? Well, this image should go some way to explaining usage but perhaps only partly! (D)S333 is the visible fleet number of the wagon in the Departmental stock? Methinks the M7 should be careful when moving away from the wagon as a spillage could have drastic results! *F.W. Hampson (ARPT)*.

Often seen shunting at the works, O2 No.30233 was one of the Eastleigh (71A) allocation during the 1950s. The 0-4-4T transferred to Eastleigh in February 1950 from Exmouth Junction (72A) and remained on the books until withdrawn in February 1958. This undated image must be early days as that SOUTHERN logo is persistently stubborn to remain on view. *K.H. Cockerill (ARPT).*

(*opposite*) L.S.W.R No.563 and LBSCR A1 No.82 BOXHILL await attention at Eastleigh on 6th October 1959. Both engines were due to be got ready for permanent exhibition at Clapham Museum but it was nearer Christmas 1960 before the 4-4-0 was dealt with. No.563 was taken by road to Clapham on 26th January 1961 with the 0-6-0T following on a later date. Both locomotives were repainted once at Clapham Museum. *Both N.W.Skinner (ARPT).*

Back in the Erecting shop where the date is now 13th June 1965 and BR Standards make-up the majority of the steam motive power inside. However, 'Rebuilt Merchant Navy' No.35003 HOLT LINE makes a nice change even though it is separated from its wheels. *N.W. Skinner (ARPT).*

A visit to the locomotive works on 30th October 1965 revealed an establishment which was very much in the throes of transition even though the Southern Region still had almost two years of main-line steam ahead of it. By now Eastleigh was the only SR locomotive works dealing with locomotive overhauls and repairs, Ashford having been turned over to wagon construction whilst Brighton closed from 1964! Present were: WC&BB: 34021 DARTMOOR, 34095 BRENTOR; MN: 35010 BLUE STAR, 35026 LAMPORT & HOLT LINE; BR Std.5: 73022.

Drewry DM: D2286; R&H DE: D2988; BR/EE DE: D3044; BR Sulzer Type 2: D5016, D5036, D5090, D5095; BRC&W Type 3: D6501, D6518, D6569, D6590; BR/EE DE: 15227; BR/EE Bo-Bo: E5009; BR/SR Co-Co: 20003.

An absence of the smaller steam locomotive types in the shops, including those regarded as the Southern Railway's own standard types, reveals a void created when hundreds of SR engines were withdrawn and scrapped as electrification, dieselisation and so-called rationalisation all combined to rid the region of its steam locomotive fleet.

Further along the shop on that same day 'Rebuilt West Country' No.34098 TEMPLECOMBE has its valve gear made ready for fine-tuning. The electric locomotive is 20003. *N.W. Skinner (ARPT).*

Below is the list of locomotives found on Eastleigh shed on that 30th day of October day in 1965. Here too we can see the gradual and not so subtle transition taking place. W - Withdrawn.

30053 W, 30071, 30926 W, 31639, 31811 W, 31842 W, 33018 W, 34036, 34037, 34046 W, 34076, 34085 W, 34108, 41287, 41294, 41313, 41319, 43147 W, 43155 W, 73016, 73043, 73086, 73111 W, 73113, 73115, 73118, 73133, 73169, 73171, 75067 W, 75068, 75076, 75077, 76011, 76016, 76019, 76053, 76060, 76061, 76062 W, 76068 W, 80015, 80016, 80065, 80083, 80132, 80137 W, 80139, 80150 W, 84014.

D2179, D2285, D2998, D3010, D3093, D3274, D6503, D6508, D6520, D6525, D6528, D6537, D6540, D6542, D6546, D6548, D6550, D6578, 15201, 15232.

An unidentified BR Standard Class 4 2-6-0 receives a Casual repair at Eastleigh circa 1960. Eastleigh was responsible for overhauling the Southern Region allocation of this class which at various times totalled over forty locomotives with Eastleigh (71A) depot housing as many as twenty of them during the lifetime of the class. From 1964 Class 4s from the London Midland Region also began to visit Eastleigh for overhauls. *Stour Valley Model Railway Club*.

'WC' No.34016 BODMIN undergoing a Heavy Intermediate overhaul in October 1954. Having run more than 309,000 miles, and now some nine years old, the Pacific was still allocated to Exmouth Junction, its initial shed from new; a transfer to Ramsgate was more than three years away and which would coincide with rebuilding. This particular locomotive is now preserved. *Stour Valley Model Railway Club*.

During a visit to Eastleigh shops, Rebuilt 'MN' No.35028 CLAN LINE reveals much of the plumbing at the front end not normally on show. The date of this image has been lost but a Light Intermediate overhaul during the summer of 1961 would fit the bill nicely – see the next image. *Stour Valley Model Railway Club.*

In June 1961 'BB' No.34078 222 SQUADRON was given a Light Intermediate overhaul at Eastleigh which would prove to be its penultimate visit to the shops prior to withdrawal in September 1964 at Exmouth Junction shed which was by then under Western Region control. Interestingly this Pacific kept the same un-modified tender - No.3328 – throughout its life. Note 'MN' No.35028 behind. *Stour Valley Model Railway Club.*

(*opposite*) Two views of soon to be preserved 'Schools' No.30926 – REPTON – stored at Eastleigh on 13th June 1965 some two-and-a-half-years since it was withdrawn. both *N.W.Skinner (ARPT)*.

Only two M7s were apparently preserved and this is one of them at Eastleigh on 13th June 1965 along with some other hardware and an unidentified Standard Class 5 – for the record No.30245 was the other preserved M7. *N.W. Skinner (ARPT)*.

No.30053 from another angle, waiting patiently for refurbishment and immortality? *N. W. Skinner (ARPT).*

Stewarts Lane (73A) N15 No.30794 SIR ECTOR DE MARIS basks in the sunshine at Eastleigh after completing a major overhaul on 7th May 1955. This 4-6-0 was one of the Eastleigh-built 'Arthurs' – 30793–30806 – put into traffic during 1926-27 in the Central (Brighton) Section of the Southern. By the spring of 1959 the N15 had transferred to Basingstoke (70D) where it was to end its days working secondary services until called to the scrapyard in August 1960. *F. W. Hampson (ARPT)*.

Some locomotives worked somewhat sedate lives during BR days and the three surviving Adams 0415 class engines were no exception. The trio were the remnants of a class of seventy-one locomotives built between 1882 and 1885 and which became some of the first victims of railway electrification when the L&SWR London suburban lines were electrified in 1916 and many of the class were withdrawn. This is No.30584 inside Eastleigh shops on 8th June 1958 receiving an Intermediate repair. The youngest of the three – the others were Nos.30582 and 30583 – our subject was built in December 1885 and the first to be withdrawn in February 1961; she was cut up later in the year. The three worked the Lyme Regis branch whereby one engine worked the branch for a week and another was spare at Exmouth Junction shed, whilst the third one was available for works visits, washouts, etc. In 1961 the branch became part of the Western Region when boundaries were redrawn. The WR thought the arrangement with the 0415 class tanks rather wasteful and returned them to the SR whilst bringing in their own Ivatt Cl.2s to work the branch. Two of the three were scrapped whilst No.30583 was preserved – not bad out of seventy-one. The story of these attractive 'Atlantic' tank engines with its many twists and turns is certainly worth a read. *C. J. B. Sanderson (ARPT)*.

It wasn't all scrapyards and negative events in BR days. This is T9 No.30284 leaving Eastleigh on the 5th May 1955 after a General overhaul and looking rather smart with that eight-wheel tender stacked high with some quality coal alongside some dross. The 4-4-0 was heading back to its home shed at Dorchester (71C) where it was a long-time resident and from where it worked until withdrawn in April 1958. The main erecting shops and boiler shop can be seen in the left background. *C. J. B. Sanderson (ARPT).*

The Erecting shop on Tuesday 28th August 1956 with the usual suspects in for overhaul or repair; one of Fratton's A1X 'Terriers' – No.32640 – displays a different lamp iron arrangement to the Brighton Works engine illustrated earlier. Note also what appears to be a spark arrester placed on the chimney. This was another of the Brighton engines which was sold to the Isle of Wight Central Railway in 1902 and which came back to the mainland in 1947 and was renumbered 2640 having been W11 NEWPORT; it has since been preserved. *Howard Forster.*

Also in the works on that August Tuesday in 1956 and just a bit further down the same bay was Brighton (75A) based H2 'Atlantic' No.32424 BEACHY HEAD. This locomotive was by now amongst the last three operational H2s with sisters 32421 SOUTH FORELAND and 32426 ST.ALBANS HEAD having been withdrawn during that August. Our subject engine did become the last of the Brighton 'Atlantics' when it was withdrawn in April 1958. Although thought was given by some towards its preservation, the more obvious ending took place a month later when No.32424 was broken up. Now, take a look at the ladder leaning against the cab of the BR Standard; those spiked strings made sure that those particular ladders didn't move too easily when someone was working on them. It must be break time as one of the seated personnel on the left is lighting up a fag. *Howard Forster.*

Stabled alongside the southern yard at Eastleigh (71A) engine shed on 28th August 1956 were these two tank engines which couldn't be more different. Nearest is former Plymouth Devonport & South Western Junction 757 class 0-6-2T No.30758 which carried the name LORD ST. LEVAN and which was now resident at Eastleigh shed since transferring from Plymouth Friary (72D) shed four months previously with sister No.30757 EARL OF MOUNT EDGECUMBE. Since its arrival the 0-6-2T had done little if any work and was now awaiting withdrawal which would take place in the following December with entry into Eastleigh scrapyard following in early 1957. Buffered up to the '757' was Adams O2 No.30177, one of a class which became synonymous with the Isle-of-Wight after their introduction to the island's railway by the Southern Railway at Grouping. The O2 was built in 1889 at Nine Elms so was eighteen years older than the six-coupled tank. Its fortunes were slightly better than the PD&SWJR engine in that it went into works for overhaul and went back into traffic for another three years. Looking at the pair it is difficult to see that the four-coupled tank weighed only three tons less than the '757' but the latter engine was built by contractors in 1907 specifically with a lighter axle-load in mind. *Howard Forster.*

The other '757' No.30757 EARL OF EDGECUMBE employed as one of the Works pilots on 28th August 1956. *Howard Forster*.

Q class No.30533 languishes on the scrap road at Eastleigh on 20th April 1963. Another one of Eastleigh's products, the 0-6-0 was withdrawn in March and would cease to exist by the end of the following month. Just twenty-five years old, this engine had been fitted with one of the wide chimneys and the multiple-jet blast pipe system. Latterly allocated to Brighton (75A), Norwood Junction (75C) had been its home for most its BR lifetime along with five other members of the class. *George Ives (ARPT).*

'700' Class 3F No.30309 didn't really look its age of sixty-six years – okay a bit of rebuilding in the 1920s might have altered a few things but basically this was the original with a superheater, extended smokebox and frames. The other thing noticeable about the 0-6-0 was the fact that it had been withdrawn some seven months prior to this image being recorded however it was scrapped just a few weeks later. Latterly allocated to Salisbury shed, it had spent the early years of BR at Feltham, a depot which always had the largest number of the class allocated. *F.W. Hampson (ARPT)*.

To finish off we present H15 No.30483 looking rather grotty – as was the norm during the period for secondary tiered engines – but nevertheless it was well proportioned especially with that eight-wheel tender. The date when this photograph was recorded was 28th August 1956 and the 4-6-0 was allocated at that time to Eastleigh shed after a spell at Nine Elms (70A) during the early years of BR. Classified from 1953 as 4P5F, they had been simply 4MT beforehand. No.30483 was withdrawn in June 1957 and broken up very soon afterwards. *Howard Forster*.